Poem Potluck

A Delightful Mix of 21 Poems

Anaya Singh

BookLeaf
Publishing

India | USA | UK

Made with ❤ on the BookLeaf Publishing Platform
www.bookleafpub.in
www.bookleafpub.com

Dedication

This book is dedicated to my **mother** and **mentor** for always supporting and encouraging me. ***Poem Potluck*** is also **dedicated to all the readers around the world** who find **true magic** in **poems.**

Preface

Welcome to **"Poem Potluck**

A delightful gathering of words, rhythm and joy. Much like a potluck dinner where everyone brings a unique dish to share, this book offers a variety of poems, each crafted to bring a smile, spark imagination and spread warmth.
Whether you're here for a laugh, a moment of wonder, or a quick escape into rhyme, you'll find something to savor.

So, dive in, explore, and let these poems brighten your day.
With joy,
Anaya

Acknowledgements

From whimsical rhythms and important messages, to
funny endings and joy giving lines, India's one of the
most amazing
poem writer, 'Anaya' spins the web of the poem history
and creates new, refreshing poems for all the bookworms
out there. A book that contains 21 mind- blowing poems.
Accompanied by an eye- catching cover illustration, the
best to go with all delightful poems.

1. Nature's Whispers

The Earth is green, the sky is blue,
Let's keep it clean for me and you.

Trees that sway, birds that sing
Nature's giving us everything!

Clean rivers flow, mountains stand tall
Many creatures, **BIG** and *small!*

The air we breathe,
The soil we live upon.

Reduce, Reuse and Recycle too,
Little things that we can do!

Protect the Earth; its our only home
Together we can, not all alone!

Let's plant a tree, pick up the waste
Making our world a better place!

"Cause every *small* step, makes a **BIG** difference."

2. The Magic of Flowers

Flowers bloom with colors bright,
Spreading joy from morning light.
Petals soft, with scents so sweet,
Dancing gently in the heat.

In the garden, side by side,
Tulips, daisies, roses wide,
Each one tells a story true,
Of the sunshine, skies so blue.

They smile in the morning breeze,
Whispering secrets with the trees.
A gift of nature, full of grace,
Brightening every single place.

So when you see a flower bloom,
Feel its magic, chase the gloom,
For every petal, every hue,
Brings a little joy to you.

3. Charming Birds

In the morning, chirping chirping!
Birds waking me up!

Parrots, pigeons, sparrows, seagulls
All are waking up!

Flying up high, in the sky
Searching for the seeds.

I wish I could, be a bird
And fly around the world!

Soaring through clouds, feeling free,
Over mountains, past the sea.

Nestling in trees, with branches wide,
On gentle winds, I'd love to glide.

Seeing sights from up above,

Filling the skies with joy and love.

From dawn to dusk, I'd fly away,
Living the dream, day by day!

4. Village VS City

In the village, skies stretch wide and clear
With cows that moo and birds that cheer.

The fields are green, the rivers gleam
Where kids run free, chasing a dream.

In the city, lights shine *oh so bright!*
With cars and buses day and night.

The buildings reach up to the sky
Where people rush and planes fly by.

In the village, quiet fills the air,
With flowers blooming here and there.

In the city, sounds never cease,
A bustling place that *never sleeps!*

"Two worlds apart, yet both have charms

The village's calm, the city's alarms.

5. Digital India

In a world of screens and light,
Digital India's shining bright.
Phones and tablets, all around,
Connecting people, sight and sound.

In the cities, in the fields,
Technology, power yields.
Learning, trading, all with ease,
Digital winds in every breeze.

Simple clicks, and lives are changed,
Dreams and futures rearranged.
In this land, a tech embrace,
Digital India's smiling face.

With an internet connection, doors open wide,
Bridging gaps from side to side.
Learning, laughter, work and play,
A world of wonder, just a click away.

"Dreams still soar, and progress shines bright,
In Digital India, united in light."

6. Childhood

In childhood days of pure delight,
The world is bright from morning to night.
With laughter ringing through the air,
Adventures find us everywhere.

We build our forts and sail our ships,
With chocolate smiles and sticky fingertips.
The simple joys, the games we play,
In endless sunshine, day by day.

The swings lift us to the sky,
As dreams and hopes soar up high.
The playground is our grandest stage,
A timeless, boundless, carefree age.

Oh, to cherish these golden years,
With magic in our laughter and cheers.
In memories, forever with light,
Childhood's charm remains in sight.

"In childhood's glow, each day's a play,
Where every moment's a bright, new day"

7. The Jungle

Deep in the jungle where the wild things grow,
A magical world puts on its show.
The trees stretch high, and the vines hang low,
And secrets hide where the rivers flow.

Monkeys swing with a cheerful chatter,
While parrots squawk in a noisy clatter.
The tiger prowls with a graceful stride,
Its golden eyes like fire that hide.

Elephants stomp with a mighty thud,
Turning the trails into pools of mud.
Snakes slither by with a silent charm,
While frogs leap high, sounding the alarm!

The fireflies dance in the velvet night,
Their glowing sparks a twinkling sight.
Cicadas hum with a buzzing tune,
Serenading the stars and the silver moon.

The jungle's alive, it's a world of song,
Where every creature belongs all along.
A symphony wild, untamed, and free,
The heart of nature, for all to see!

8. Gender Equality

Girls build towers, *boys* paint skies,
Both can dream and reach for highs.
Girls can lead and *boys* can bake,
All can choose the paths they take.

Boys can dance and *girls* can race,
Each can find their special place.
Girls can code and *boys* can sew
Together they can learn things new!

Boys can sing and *girls* can climb,
Each with their choices and ways!
Hand in hand, let's walk the way,
For a world where we all can play!

"Girls and boys side by side,
Different choices but they have rights."

9. What If?

What if the moon could talk at night,
And told us tales of its silver light?
What if the stars were sugar and spice,
Sprinkled across a celestial slice?

What if the trees could sing and dance,
Shaking their leaves in a leafy prance?
What if the oceans sang a tune,
Serenading the world beneath the moon?

What if the clouds were made of fluff,
And pillows rained when storms got rough?
What if the wind could whisper a rhyme,
Telling the secrets of space and time?

What if your shadow had things to say,
And followed you chatting all through the day?
What if the clocks decided to freeze,
Letting us live in moments with ease?

What if the world was upside down,
And fish wore hats while sharks wore crowns?
What if the grass tickled your feet,
And giggled aloud in the summer heat?

What if the world was full of surprise,
And magic lived in all our eyes?
What if we dreamed and let it be,
A world of wonders for you and me?

10. Cultural Festivals

The drums are pounding, feet take flight,
Dances honor traditions bright.
Lanterns glow with ancient art,
Cultural festivals warm the heart!

Songs of heritage fill the air,
Stories told with pride and care.
Savor dishes from distant lands,
A melting pot of skilled hands.

Parades of costumes, bold and grand,
Crafts that speak of every strand.
Cultures blending, voices sing,
The festival unites everything!

Flags of nations, colors gleam,
A world connected, like a dream.
In this vibrant, sacred space,
We celebrate each culture's grace!

11. My Birthday is Here!

Today's the day, it's finally here,
A time for laughter, love, and cheer!
With cake to eat and games to play,
Hooray, hooray—it's my birthday!

Candles glowing, wishes made,
Friends and fun that never fade.
Balloons rise high, the streamers gleam,
It feels just like a magical dream.

Gifts are opened, surprises delight,
Laughter and smiles from morning to night.
The joy I feel, so warm and true,
A day of love in every hue.

As stars come out and night draws near,
I treasure the moments so bright, so clear.
A perfect day, so full of glee,
The happiest day just for me!

12. The Joy of School

School is a place where dreams take flight,
Where we learn by day and dream at night.
Books and pencils, desks in a row,
So many wonders waiting to show!

In math, we solve each tricky riddle,
In music, we sing or play the fiddle.
Science unveils the world's great plan,
History tells us where it began.

Friends are near with laughs to share,
Kindness and teamwork fill the air.
Lessons and games, a perfect mix,
With every day, new goals to fix.

School is a treasure, a gift so bright,
Filling our minds with knowledge and light.
So let's embrace each learning rule,
And celebrate the joy of school!

13. I Wish... (No. 1)

I wish I were a rabbit,
To hop all around.
I'd be cute and furry,
And live underground.

When I'd see the hunter,
I will not make a sound.
I'd skip and dodge, and hide myself,
From the Great Greyhound.

14. I Wish... (No. 2)

I wish I were a book,
I'd say don't go on looks.

I'd spread knowledge everywhere,
And make poverty disappear.

With letters that are **BOLD**, *Italic* and Underlined,
I'd be a non-living divine.

With every turning page,
I'd act like a sage.

Page numbers and chapter's tittle,
I'd say to others that cleanliness is vital!

Hearing people say, *"Oooh* and *Aaah!"*
But I'd not listen to *"Blah-blah-blah!"*

I really wish I was a book,
But being a human is just as good!

15. I Wish... (No. 3)

I wish I was a magical bird,
A creature that is never heard.

I'd fly up above the clouds, with wings spread out wide,
To the big moon, oh so bright!

With a small pointed beak and rainbow feathers,
I'll wear magical slippers made of leather.

I'd like to explore pine trees,
And fly above the seven seas.

I'd live on the tallest mountains,
Drink water from a fountain.

I'd pick and eat up the seeds,
And create a pet with random beads.

A magical pet to accompany me,
I'd name it, *"Unicorni Ki."*

16. Limerick- A Girl's Mistake

There was a girl who made a mistake,
She sat on her grandma's plate of cake.
She felt cold in her dress,
And checked the frosting mess,
Then laughed and said, "It is for fun's sake.

17. Limerick- Habit of a Girl

There was a young girl with a habit,
She munched and crunched like a rabbit.
On carrots she'd dine,
In the sun she'd recline,
And munch till she squeaked, "I must have it!"

18. Limerick- A Girl who Likes to Read

There once was a girl named Marie,
Whose nose was in books constantly.
From fiction to lore,
She'd always want more,
Her mind sailed on each story's sea!

19. (Haiku-1) Summer's Playful Heat

It's hot in summer,
But I want to play outside,
Having lots of fun.

The sun shines so bright,
Sweat drips as I run around,
Laughing with my friends.

Ice cream cools my cheeks,
Splashing in the pool feels nice,
Joy fills every day.

20. (Haiku-2) Lockdown

Stop! Shut down, lock up.
Wash hands, get vaccinated,
Beware! It's virus.

Masks shield breaths of life,
Distance keeps us safe, apart,
Hope whispers, "Hold on."

Spring will bloom again,
Healing winds will sweep the earth,
Together, we'll rise.

21. (Haiku-3) Rainbow Dreams

Colors arch the sky,
Dreams unfold in golden light,
Whispers soft as sighs.

Step across the hues,
Magic flows beneath your feet,
Hope is in the air.

At the rainbow's end,
Treasures glow within your heart,
Joy begins to bloom.